MW01293363

This book belongs to:

____

Made in the USA
Las Vegas, NV
04 December 2020

11985316R10066